'Just

PASSING
THROUGH des

That's love
on the run'

Bought this ages
ago, as you'll see
and just got round
to passing it on –
all the way from
the US of A.

Olivia
x

PASSING THROUGH

JOHN TRIPP

United States distributor
DUFOUR EDITIONS, INC.
Booksellers and Publishers
Chester Springs, PA 19425
215-458-5005

POETRY WALES PRESS
1984

POETRY WALES PRESS
56 PARCAU AVENUE, BRIDGEND,
MID GLAMORGAN

British Library Cataloguing in Publication Data

Tripp, John
    Passing through.
    I. Title
    821'.914   PR6070.R47

ISBN 0-907476-35-X

Cover Design: Cloud Nine Design.

*The publisher acknowledges the financial support of the Welsh Arts
Council*

Typeset by Afal, Cardiff
Printed in 11pt Goudy Old Style
by
Antony Rowe Ltd., Chippenham.

Contents

Acknowledgements

Certain of these poems have appeared in
*The Anglo-Welsh Review, Arcade, Element Five, Poetry
Wales, Planet* and *Ocarina (Bombay)*.

Folly before midnight

They tucked us away in a late
late slot: after the clowns
and before the weather forecast.
The inquisitor was a reserve
office boy, ungroomed for stardom
where his peers climbed to the light.

Even the cameramen yawned
more than usual. We were only
a couple of grey scriveners
wheeled in across the Dyke.
The boy gave us fifteen minutes
to say nothing, between the silences.

I could predict it. He took the stage
versions of our backward tribe
nourished by jesters since they invented
Welsh Rarebit. Weariness came over me
for the disappearance of history,
for another who did no homework.

We could see him almost nodding off.
'Thank you gentlemen' he said.
I tried, but could not resist
'Indeed to goodness look you butt'
as he shuffled his papers
and the red light went out.

Zeal of the convert

Bluebottles dive and buzz
against a porthole in The Trappist Arms.
When somebody moves, a mongrel
growls from the mat. I order a pint
in English. 'Don't speak that heathen
tongue here,' he says, the one just come
from a Saxon campus. He is not
joking. (For an instant the terrible image
blazes, as I see myself catapulted
out of a culture.) Then I lift two fingers
in a dismissive V, and wonder:
If we were dumb, would we be less Welsh?

In Othello's, Soho

Cutlery clinks as the glittering editor snaps
his briefcase shut, shoots forward
his crisp cuffs with the big silver
ice-axe links. His friend droops: he's done
too many readings, he hears the fading
of applause. The silken editor favours
sweetbreads with cinnamon and a carafe
of Mateus. Gritty, provincial, I bend
to this gourmet, to his impeccable
taste as his slim fingers touch
the carafe funnel and he simpers
compliment on the Celtic upsurge.
His friend dozes, hazed from recitation,
his poems small as cherrystones.

Reality in Ludlow

I

In De Grey's long coffeehouse
I took tea and éclairs
among genteel border matrons.
An eccentric in cape and deerstalker
jogged by with his pony and gig
as four Welsh Blacks skirted a grid.

(Shift that kiosk, that telegraph
pole, and you could see
the archers coming back from Bosworth.)
Above the courts and mews
Tudor and Georgian leaned on one another,
black-and-white between rose-red.

Under its fort
the old town was silent, caught
in a time-stop, its story
not Welsh or English, its spirit
leaked down a ditch between two lands
where twisted magnates and marcher lords
carved up tomorrow on a map.

Harmless only in sleep,
their lives were shorter
and nastier, their manner pitiless
beyond telling, a chill indifference
the fatal weed. Forgotten men
are earthed along the whole line
from Wem to the banks of Wye.

I bought a guide
raddled with bias, with praise
for power on horseback
and the greed of satraps.
Here the rabbles were sent
packing, bootless. It was a hinge
to a colony, the key kings turned
to slide their bacillus through.

II

At the Angel I had steak-
and-kidney, plum duff with claret.
I felt like John Bull, union-jacked
around the girth, and spoilt with favour.
My concept of history and imperial damage
shattered on the third goblet,
for no horsemen passed the mullion
with lances and pennants, no platoon
of foot with slung muskets.

All I saw was a bus
of pensioners from Neath, a truck
going home to Skewen,
their sources painted on the side.
Even the solitary waiter,
sagging with boredom as he brought
the dish of plum duff,
said he came from Rhoose.

Ploughman

'You may not get a chance
to see this again,' the correspondent
from Power Farming said to me.

Near Builth I watched him
slowly carve up a plot
in neat straight grooves, doing
a precision high-cut run
with the polished furrow slices
gleaming like metal.
He turned through an exact angle
of a hundred-and-thirty degrees
without breaking, and packing firm
against the previous slice.
It was the true straightness
of the lines you had to see,
as if he steered along white paint.

The shires stopped on a tuppence
when he yelled Whoa!
They stopped with one foot in the air
and put it back, not forward.
He fussed and tuned his ship
when he felt a slight change
of texture, or the horses leaned
into a breeze. He did an acre
a day, walking ten miles
behind the big patient team.
A really bad error was visible
in soil or crop for a year.
His craft seemed timeless, and beautiful.

He was one of the last
of his skill. I'm glad I saw it
before his plough went to a museum.

Scratch Farmer

We argued. Running poor land had to be
about slick methods. I think his belief
was in equal ration of sun and rainfall.
On a bog backholding behind some engine sheds
survival meant pigs, lean pork to compete.
Flop-hatted in dripping heat, he stooped to it.

He kept the sty as clean as a horse box;
a few geese fattened on corn in the orchard
where windfalls made head-blowing cider.
He remembered when the freight came through
and the overdug quarries were full of men,
when people bought pork with a peach-fed look.

The scratched patch reverted to dock and nettle.
A worn cog in the country wheel, tardily he creaked
into debt, sold his shack and pigs and geese.
At fifty he limped down to the rackety coast
to a caravan slum on the candyfloss strip
and stirred vats in a fish-and-chip trough.

Walnut Tree Forge

My father shod horses in the sun
while I threw old shoes at an iron pin.
From the bank of the canal I saw
a kingfisher dive like a blue-green streak
clean through the water and out again
with lunch in its beak, then glide
to its fish-boned hole in the bank.

My father would look up from his work
and lean against the door to rest
from the bending, the weight on his back
of a shire, big and restless in the heat,
that tested all his muscles and skill.
He would wipe his brow with a rag.
'Did you see a kingfisher, then?' I nodded.

He never welcomed the big horses
made for show, all rump and heavy
with the spoilt pride of their runners,
shone to a tantrum and cockade gloss
for anything but work. These gave him
a rough hour of shifting and fret,
too pampered by the hands of others.

It was labour to him, one more task
for a pound, the ponies coming in a string
on a good day. To me it was freedom
from arithmetic, as golden time used up
so easily. There were just the two of us,
the ring of the shoes hitting the pin,
and a kingfisher, and a shire, in the long-ago sun.

R.S. Thomas

He belongs there
on a peninsula, an inset
off the main map. I looked
at his face, the character
etched on it, reflecting his
structures. I have never
fully grasped him, blinking
at his attack on the machine,
the slick tractor like life
putting on too much speed;
his groan against the hook
of a deity, hiding from him
among stones. Yet I feel
a slight awe, uncomfortable
in reverence. This lean
priest, spare and taut
as his lines — the words
short, clean, made to wipe
away muddle. He sits
writing by a north cliff
watching aliens in the lost
parishes; shut to interlopers
drawn to his remoteness
like flies; using his pen
to argue with God, to put
pride back into the sick
Welsh hag. We have gladly
shared his offering — the bleak
cracked love and wan
disgust — his
               'bread of truth'.

Second coming

All was prepared for the event:
pennants flew in the streets,
balloons let loose on the mountain,
his portrait hung in the shops;
the clothes lines were taken down
and the camera crews lined up.
Folk-groups stood on a hillside
and girls wearing rainbow sashes
beat on drums. We waited....
For miles the roads were jammed
with cars and trucks and buses.
His steak supper lay on the grill
and wine decanted. The pubs brimmed
with schooners of ale, and corks
popped in the best hotel.
We waited, shivering in the wind.

He entered from the south —
bearded, dusty, tired and travel-stained
in an Alfa-Romeo. The men shouted
and some of the women wept.
Stray dogs from slums and allotments
followed in behind the wheels.
He cruised down the main street
looking lazily to left and right.
He stopped on the edge of town
staring at the bland councillors
who fiddled with their chains of office,
and the priests, who looked flummoxed.
Then he really put his foot down and raced
to the top of the hill. He turned, just
once, twisting in his seat, and put up
two fingers to the sky....

Connection in Bridgend

In the bus café, drinking tea, I watch
nothing happening in Bridgend.
I mean, there is rain, some shoppers
under canopies, tyres sloshing them
from the gutters. Otherwise not much.

(Do those Pakistanis feel the cold?
What are they doing in Bridgend?
How did they land here, and those lost
Sikhs and Chinamen?
I am sorry for them, they look bereft.)

In the café a young mother is being given
stick by her two boys. They want Coke
and her baby cries for no reason
unless he's seen enough of Bridgend.
I feel an odd kinship with him.

At last my bacon sandwich is done;
it was something to look forward to,
slicing a minute's delight into the murk.
Balancing the plate, I hold the sad babe
while his mother fetches the Coke.

Then a one-armed paperseller comes in
with a strip of frayed ribbons on his coat.
He wants to tell me his story,
so I listen while the baby sobs
and his brothers suck straws.

An hour ago, I was alone; now
there are six. Even the café-owner
squeezes out a smile. We are in it
together, until the last buses go out.
One by one they leave the bays.

Ashes on the Cotswolds

He asked me to accompany him
to collect his sister-in-law's ashes
in Southampton, and then scatter them
somewhere on the Cotswolds.
She and her husband had honeymooned there.
His brother couldn't face it, he said.

It was a Saturday. We had to be there
before noon, when the place closed
(weren't people cremated on Saturdays?)
He owned a powerful Humber Hawk
and he drove like Fangio
to reach Southampton in time.

Was it the right urn? How
could we tell? We stopped for lunch
in Salisbury, and over the roast lamb he said:
'My sister-in-law's on the back seat of that car.'
Then we headed for the range
to keep his promise to his brother.

Somewhere near Cleeve Hill
he took the lid off the urn
and threw the ashes into the wind.
They blew back on us
as I tried to take a photograph
to send to his grieving brother.

The ashes disappeared on the wind
and were dust on our clothes.
We shook it off, and I took
a photo of the urn in the grass.
As we say on these occasions,
it was what she would have wanted.

Looking for Viriamu Lewis

'You'll get it in Oriel.'
They all say that.
It is a luxurious paperback feast
in cool white rooms, but I cannot
find the essays of Thomas Pratt.

'Do you stock Viriamu Lewis?'
'Who?'
'Never mind.'
I end downstairs in a corner
lost among the movie books
with overrated roly-poly Hitchcock,
Orson Welles and his miraculous kind.

It is always thus: I ferret
for dead obscure scribes
and finish with Harlow and Marilyn Monroe.
Look, here is a picture of Peter Finch
                    (the other Peter Finch),
Tony Curtis (the other...), and Clara Bow.

I am back in the dark again
at the Rialto in Whitchurch
with Gold Flake and sweets,
Alan Ladd tilting back his hat.
Who needs Thomas Pratt or Viriamu Lewis
when Erich von Stroheim is here
with Mitchum and Raquel Welch
who performed such celluloid feats?

There in the silence of Oriel
I devour the movie books —

Fassbinder, Renoir, Visconti, and Lean.
Like billiards and booze
it is evidence of a misspent youth.
Glamour, Excitement, Romance!
Anything to escape the truth.

Away

Another gig done. Another hotel.
Cells in the two-star range
always look much the same:
biscuit or mustard-coloured
with nothing on the walls,
nothing that can be unscrewed.
Cold, temporary, anonymous —
for people on the run
with money in their pocket.

I plug the kettle into a socket
to make a cup of Nescafé.
What's useful is to know
how light you can travel
with a Pan-Am bag: toothbrush
and tube, pyjamas, spare
shirt, linen and socks;
a tin of coffee, spirit flask,
aspirin and a couple of books.

(I think of other rooms
where solitaries sleep tonight:
the commercial pushing his special
line, the engineer on his way
to a port, already missing his wife.
Everywhere the silences descend
in the night of provincial towns,
everywhere the lights go out
on solitaries in transit.)

Sometimes I cannot remember
the name of the town I am in,
let alone the blank hotel.
Years of trains and buses
and their hopeless connections
have dulled my edge.
What I choose to remember
is that I do it, that still
somehow it is worth doing.

Tonight I read twenty poems
to a crowd of twenty.
It went as these things go —
reaching out for a moment
with a break for tea and cake.
I cannot sleep, thinking
about the next one, somewhere
in Flint. To pass the time
I start to write this...

Seat of learning

'Plato banned poets from his Republic
as liars, too dangerous to live'
the grey corduroy professor said.
He tilted his crystal decanter
in a last stand for the baroque.
He only liked poets who were dead.

There were no dreaming turrets
here, no ivy quads or plaqued
cloisters. Only functional barns.
Out of aeroplane hangars
and formica canteens, lovely girls
strode towards their Volkswagons.

The Martians had been, and Lowell,
a trickle of fashionable mandarins
dissecting the bones of Hardy.
But where were the young Platos
discoursing in the plastic piazza
on six schooners of sherry?

I read inside an airline terminal
all concourse, parquét and glass,
padded against wild intention.
The words of an old language
floated off into space, alone,
lost in acoustic perfection.

On Bosworth Field

The Dormobile's wipers swished through
a screen of rain, pelting across the fields.
This one looked just like the others, green.
The sly driver yawned, offering us
wild-boar plastic necklets
'as worn by Dick the Third.'

'I remember the film' a woman said.
So did I: Henry, on his knees
praying in a Rhondda accent, behind him
   a tent, banners, and many extras;
Richard screaming for his horse, then
twitching in his throes on the turf
   and a tin crown stuck on Henry's head;
the swords ringing through the last
   collision of the Roses.

(I thought: These commotions of history,
this speechless flux that swallows us;
these stones in the corners of fields,
this fight for our memory of dead kings.)

'Time to go' the driver said, still yawning.
The blood must have been everywhere
   on that summer day ...
My boot disturbed a crisp-bag and Coke-bottle.
Then there was a drumming on the air
like invisible hooves; it came
from a corner of the Field,
from a long battle flag
streaming and thrumming in the wind.

'I remember the film' the woman said.

Good Friday

I purchase my small Easter offerings:
a Black Magic egg for my friend,
six hot cross buns for my father,
an uplift card to a pious aunt.
These are customary over the years
since the loss of our stiffer
rituals — the morning prayer, the fish
at dinner, the evening walk
with Bibles to the long sermon.

On the wind I hear the chimes
from Ararat, calling its remnant.
Another house opens at noon
packed with lapsed Christians
who drink swiftly against the clock
and stay on past the dead taps.
I fool myself into some pretence
of joy, pressing down a hollowness
and not knowing why it comes.

Hours go by.... I spend the whole day
watching a screen, reading old papers
and drinking tea. Then I put out
the milk bottle, and feed the cat.
Another Good Friday draws to a close,
tied completely to the temporal.
I switch off the lamps. As usual
there is something seriously missing,
but I do not know what it is.

Bitter morsel

Together we burrowed above quadrangles,
digging out the perfidy of kings
and the tracks of feckless clerics
crawling in a slime of dominion.

History with its twists and dead ends,
its tardiness to yield the truth,
slowed our clocks in useless rummaging.
There was a lesson here, if we could learn it.

When she linked my fingers, I pondered
our own acts of treason, as we drop
into false alliances. Even my thought
formed like an essay, precise and detached.

Release from entrapment was the aim
to stop her ivy clinging, to pursue
sweet knowledge in some solitary drum
where the chaos was my own making.

Dalliance capered on, through a summer
of smoky functions awash with wine
and riddled with hurt. Communication
chopped itself down to silence.

'Goodbye then' at the train. I would come to know
the insignificance of kings and clerics
against the warmth of our couplings,
the blaze of the living moment.

Alliances

I am reading a chapter
on the Easter Rising in Dublin
when the telephone rings: Dinner at 8,
could I come? It will be elegant
in a house on Rhiwbina Hill
with patriots in their green enclave.

(We met on the blue diesel
between Didcot and Swansea
over high tea, their politics locking
into my own. It is simple
to clinch to your opposites
in the warmth of a shared creed.)

What shall I wear tonight?
Appear decent, not to enter
like some troublemaker in denim
or worn cords. I choose my biscuit
linen suit and Louis Philippe shirt.
It has come to this.

Hypocrisy smirks at me
in the glass as I knot my tie;
spaghetti and wine by candlelight
and the conversation of unrest
as we grumble past midnight
stranded on the barricades of talk.

Is there honey still for tea?

A perfect June day in Bath
where Somerset play Sussex
by the Avon. On the boundary
blue-and-white striped marquees
and the odd panama. A creak of wheels
as the sight-screen is moved a fraction.
Strawberries and cream, white figures
in a stiff ballet on the green, and the click
of a ball taking the edge.

If you filmed the scene
it would come out sepia, unchanging
but for a black fast bowler
pounding in from the Pulteney end.

I close my eyes. The pacemen
are still in the Indies, and Rupert Brooke
has come on, using slow left-arm spin.
Then some young subalterns from King's
wearing toy swords and pips on their sleeves
reappear with the fairest girls
slender as stems, who laugh and twirl parasols,
then clap gently when a wicket falls.

Everything is as it should be,
not a single black plaque in the chapels
or the long solitude of widows
and spinsters. Nothing has yet come
to hurt them, under the sun blazing in the sky
on a perfect June day by the Avon.

Passing through

I

Above the reservoir, my friend and I
picnic from a hamper like two provincials
in a French print. We watch
cherry sails on small boats
with little figures in them —
distant specks on calm water.

A solitary fishes from a skiff at the rim,
oblivious to the racers waiting for a breeze
on a June day of tropic heat,
of lemon light when the sun
warms us like some kind reward,
doing its duty at last.

Below on a wooded slope
a couple flick cakecrumbs to the birds
hopping close, domestic for a moment,
sharing this hour with us.
They come almost to the hand
competing for scraps in a free restaurant.

II

I absorb the scene, a fragment of harmony,
squinting through glasses at those far dots,
knowing it will never be repeated
exactly as it is today.
We try to preserve the cherished
but the sift of time dissolves it.

My friend, the endearment I feel for her
(especially now in her Venetian boater with a blue strip),
those red sails and small figures, the sun
spoiling us, the young couple
and the birds blend together
for a while, then pass . . .

It is not simply drift
but a severance too sudden, unlooked-for —
a thin wire of love soon snapped.
Even these images will crumble
as a poor reminder of this day —
transient, heartbreaking, gone . . .

Let me linger here above the reservoir
to keep something only for a minute,
to hold what passes like quicksilver,
I have an instinct to preserve
which seems to rely on loss.
It is the loss that is insupportable.

Whitsun at Prinknash

I

I remember when they came here
in a distant winter of snow and ice
with cattle and sheep lost under drifts.
The monks humped their goods on a farm cart
down to the slapping water and onto a barge
towed by a chugging outboard over Caldey Sound,
then rattled by truck along country roads
to a retreat in a hunting lodge.
Twice a week through the razor months
a boat bumped the freezing quay;
nine hours from Tenby to Gloucester
a community shifted from island to hill.

II

Now they keep an enclosure
close to the comforts of secular man.
Outside the old lodge, bramble spreads
through a garden, ivy smothers its walls
shored up with timber splays; a tile slips,
cracking in the mossed gutter.

Inside are mildewed remains
from half-a-century ago:
plain bowls and spoons, tin mugs,
a potter's wheel with creaking pedal
worn thin by the instep, a green wafer
and wine bottle on the floor.
Chill damp mixes with paraffin fumes,

a whiff of hospital carbolic.
A portrait of Bloody Mary tilts
on a wall, a Tudor rose bedded
in a rafter, a cavalier's head cut
on a mullion, and the Stuart arms crowned
on a stair. All the dead alliances
of Rome and martyred kings.

In a shop I buy a flawed cup
with a handle-shaped like a salmon.
'It is imperfect, as we are'
the bald monk says, profoundly.
I keep my camera locked, my respect intact
as the brothers in their off-white cloaks
pace with open books on the unmown lawns
muttering the tracts that strut their faith.

One of them stumps to clap up the chimes
to a full octave, hanging on a rope
in the belfry. The racket
is incredible, buzzing my 'drums.
Slouched against a car bonnet
I feel out of place, a lumpy interloper
with the world's stain on him, a seedy
delegate of the temporal.

The random and the accidental
that link us, the destinies
on our calenders, have drifted these men
into their solitude and silence;
history does not unnerve these gentle
Benedictines. I watch them stroll

into Vespers — so far from the start
of their story, where the meaning
conceals itself, yet still deep
in the puzzle that has brought them
to an English hilltop.

Irish passage

'Romantic Ireland's dead and gone
It's with O'Leary in the grave.' — Yeats

1 Landing

We were churned on the voyage out.
The stabilisers of a motorship
are useless against a high swell
heaving her up and down
on the last knots from Swansea to Cork.

In Moore's the yawning dregs
of a film junket drooled
over French skill, their scoop
of awards. The timeless Irish
looked at them and smiled.

I ate alone in the fancy grill
where a movie star and his blonde
shared duck and Bollinger. Nobody
wanted his autograph, nobody
surrendered to his glamour.

From the roof I saw the quays
where pillagers came and went
through centuries, leaving their stain
and charity on a ramshackle port.
The lights trailed away to a distant pinpoint.

It was time to go. I laid out my map
of the South — one place on earth
where a poor battered spirit could mend

itself, and forget things as they were.
It was my second home, across the sea.

2 Requiem in Tralee

'The sons o' doom came here,'
said the old republican in the dust
of Costello's. He looked as wild as Connemara.
Across the street were twin rusted guns
in remembrance of the military dead,
and the ruin of an Anglican church
to remind us of the imperial past.

An argument of steel and blood
was closed. I told the old fighter this,
but I knew he would sooner believe
Jesus Christ had just entered Tralee.
(The sepia of that turbulence
was still fixed in his mind
as if only then he had lived
for some dream that had gone.)

'These people forget,' the old man said.
I nodded, envying them, licking the head
off my Guinness. Through smoky glass I saw
the chromium beefburger joints and the last
piece of England in a noble thoroughfare
where the fleeting visitors walked
with the careless inheritors of a dream.

3   Listowel

Donkeys, looking wan at their role
in the world, still pull milk churns.
Shopkeepers close their doors
when a funeral passes. No one
fawns, or scrabbles at your wallet.

It is a fine tomorrow town
where they are glad to get through today
without rumpus. I owed a grocer
exactly a guinea: 'Ah, give it tomorrow.'
He had never seen me before.

'You will not want to pay
such a price' the haberdasher-lady
said, 'but it's made by the hand.'
On a wall of her Edwardian box
hung the suffering Christ.

(Does their dusty religion
give them grace, or a natural
goodness? Have their priests
preserved what we lost?
I saw decency, but no fear.)

Sunday-best Catholics pour
from the Mass and into the bars
bursting the streets from end to end.
Fifty-two bars and a racecourse,
like a wastrel's glimpse of paradise.

4   Mizen Head

Near the sea, a rusty plaque on a railing
says here is a pit full of coffinless dead
buried at the height of the Hunger.
Families starved in those roofless shacks
as the last priest gave them his blessing
within the sight of the Boston clippers.

There is no dwelling for miles —
a way of life wiped out
as if it had never been. No testimony
to a solution much simpler than guns
when a potato crop failed
and a few cold hearts did the rest.

Atlantic winds howl across the point
and the marshes, emptied of life
since that season when the earth
yielded nothing, while far away
others blandly waited
for a calamity to solve itself.

Some people cling to the shoreline,
living off the land and water,
a luckless scrape till dusk comes in.
I thought of that plaque by the pit
when a comely young waitress brought me
a piece of fresh salmon from the sea.

5   Patriots at Dingle

I came through flat trench country
of peat bogs lined by the cutters
to a strip of sand on a Kerry cape.
There was only the sea before America.

Distant music brought me
down twisting lanes to the bars
disguised as grocers' shops: the 'Paddy' tap
behind the bacon slicer and potato sack.

Pipes, fiddles, flutes and drums
were playing out Ireland's Past —
song, jig, stout and whiskey
to the Famine and the Troubles.

Fishermen coming off the smacks
sang with the patriots:
together they made the link,
a comradeship of misfortune.

'Try the poteen' someone said. 'It goes
down your throat like a torchlight procession.'
The country was full of illicit stills
but nobody would tell me the secret.

Then a pegleg blew dust off his bible —
The Struggle in West Cork — and the album
of Easter creaked across the floor
like forgotten lantern slides.

It was more Irish than a bad film.
You had to look closely to see
the sadness beyond the singing
and jokes, the gaps in the photograph.

These were the last survivors
of a tragedy, the brave green
Republic raising the poor skull
of Pearse, drowning in memories.

It was a kind of joy, this late
simplicity of regret, the shift
backward to shared loss
where none of us felt alone.

Then the car was heading towards Cork
where time ran out on the estuary.
I could not bring myself to say goodbye
to those I would not see again.

6   Return to Cork

The last time? Pictures fade
in the museum of my mind
here at Moore's as the fine porter
and Jamesons go down. Once I rode light
around places with names like Inch
and Mallow, Bantry, Ballybunion, Tralee
to come through to the bridges of Cork
and rooms above shattered distilleries.

Ireland. History's mark on it
made this tumbledown city, sprawled
in a corner, grandly hoping
for a continental elegance on the sea.
The centuries of the stranger
are in England's sad print on the tall
crumbled Georgian, between strips
of backwater slapping on rotting planks.

I love the shabbiness of it
belonging to itself and no other
since that day the tricolour flew
when the occupiers steamed away
down that narrow inlet to the sea.
Some fulfillment from the wreckage
endures in their singleness,
in the freedom of their ways.

At Moore's I feel the cold finger
of a visit nearing its end, the promises
that send me home. Now young Stack
and Tom Sullivan, descended from distant
republicans, deal the last cards

off a worn deck. Soon I pack and leave
this dignity they fought for
to board the ferry. I watch the lamps
of Cobh and the hulk of St. Patrick's
slip away from us in the night
as we slide through the long inlet
and out into the open sea....

Welsh amnesia

Grandad used to relate
what blew at Senghenydd, in detail
finer than the accident-inspector's.
We heard, remembered, passed on
the worst narrative of the coalfield.

I thought Wales was just its black south
from Rhymney looping west to Dowlais —
a strip of minerals everyone wanted.
From my uncles I rushed to transmit
bits of history to others, a Morse-tapper
fanning out in the bleak school.

Who could forget Senghenydd
burned across the mind
like Passchendaele, like the flicker
of a pegleg with a tray
                on the Plaza steps?
The three brass balls of the pawnbroker
creaking on a swivel in the wind?
The miner with a wax face
laid out with arms folded
glimpsed through a front-room window?

It was so quiet: no Irish turbulence
here, only silence in the towns, calamity
without guns, matriarchs broken by loss,
a whole generation passing
unconsidered, too brave to whimper.
A piece of history under wraps.

We migrated to West Bromwich and Slough,
minions on the oily pittance.
Years rattled by, fewer remembered
or cared to remember, erasing the past
as one would wipe a tape.
                    Walking without our shadow.

Ships came in and went out,
dumping junk on the quays;
engines puffed across the viaducts
dragging yesterday's waste.
Links snapped in the miners' library
and dust settled on the monuments.
In Tylorstown a schoolboy yawned
when I showed him the casualty list.
Who looked at the albums fading
on that chronicle of distress?
I stood on a corner in Nantgarw
gasping in the icy wind
and holding an empty notebook.

Now the young historians come
to catch the last voice
before it dies in Senghenydd....

Grandad, we are losing our memory.

Death of a father

(for T.C.)

'It was the best thing for him'
said the unconcerned, wishing to avoid
details, knowing that thing is the worst.
A malign terminus puts words
chilling as ice into our heads.

My friend wanted his grief to end.
He kept seeing his father
tap out the dottle from his pipe
on the black hob, then turn
to ask what was for supper.

Years later, he still missed him.
(They had been more like brothers
with only Time tilting its axe.)
He misjudged the hung dust
of sorrow, how it lingers
in rooms, on a road or beach,
at the edges of celebration.
What we see is how they looked
and laughed, the way they walked
towards us, their arms opened wide.

Armistice Day '77, Honiton

The two minutes' silence was cut to one
that November day; it was a busy world.
By chance, on my way to a gig
I walked into a ceremony of six
in the rain: crosses in a ring, and the poppies soaked.

Down two sides of the slab were names
linked to this piece of England — the sound
of country stock grown old in duty
and the acceptance of pointless loss.
Names going back to Minden and before.

(Were these the only ones left
to remember their dead?
Already sixty seconds were lopped
off any dignity. Would their children
forget, as I had forgotten?)

No more came. On some other day
I might have felt an interloper
marring their ritual. At eleven o'clock
the men took off their hats
and we all bowed our heads.

A minute in the rain in a country town
may whisper the whole grief of history.
Picture a knot of seven around that block,
the red wet poppies, and for just a moment
a complete and utter silence in the world.

Apprehension at Stratford

Merriment lasts as long as a nightcap
and the journey to my Tudor room
under strutted beams. Not a thought
seems out of trim, or tilts
toward much but the paltry
until I fret at the sad Dane
and ponder again that chronicle of blood,
the twists of a sick prince
who jerks our pity.
         He sounds like gospel
on the darker side of us, unswerved
by mellow dolts twittering to heaven.
I seize his tortured, eloquent word —
this story mumbled by a cretin
signifying little, and the sorrows
drooping in platoons.
         Forever in black
as if life itself was a funeral
to a backdrop of artillery and drums
with purple plumes nodding on the horses
and pennants thrumming in the wind;
his lonely notions and turbulent dreams
still racking us in bleak soliloquy
as our own griefs and follies mount.

In the room I raise a fat tumbler
of amber warmth, hoping to stifle
the unease. It is hard to believe
some scrivener of genius can penetrate this fog
four centuries on.
         But here in my cell
of a velvet hotel in an ancient town at winter

swiftly the feeling builds
with dark Hamlet the sly trigger —
that cold accustomed distress
when we are lost in our solitary enclosure,
in the reticence of sorrow....

I switch on the apricot lamp
and the screen for company,
waiting for something to pass.

Who could give it a name,
this old hollowness tinged with pity
mounting its attack through flickering images
and the shift of innocence
as baffled nobility might have named it
once on the turrets of Elsinore
before he fell through history?

The climate kept me indoors
remembering more reckless days.
Soon my typing quarto had gone
so I used the backs of bills;
only one biro functioned
then the dictionary fell apart.
Ideas dissolved in my notebook.

('Keep going' they wrote. 'Don't quit
now. Salvage something from the wreck.
This country isn't finished yet.'
All right for them, in their mountain
fastnesses, untouched by southern blight.)

As doubt dribbled down to sloth
and the toast burnt, the soup boiled over,
I thought it was time to stop.
Dreams had kept me bolt upright for years.
On a bitter Monday morning in March
the fire went out in my belly.
Outnumbered, I surrendered with bad grace.

Tintern

I

The Beaufort is lit up
for a junket; I hear laughter
and the tempo for a jig.
Looking down at the broken
Abbey, crumbling on its lawns,
I think of a long-dead poet
who built an elevated sermon
here, dreamy in the change
and dust of his century.

Under trees strung with lights
the drums and laughter fade
as a chill spikes the air.
There is another summer night
coming in across the river
and fields — slowly, tardily,
as if giving us a moment to see
the day turn to dusk. Then the revels
explode, slicing my gloom.

II

The weight of these ancient
enclosures! heavy with reminders
of flux, sagging under ivy and moss
but still filling page on page
of one doubter's quest.
Through the last of the old
green districts, these frail arches
and open naves drew me, as if there
I would find what was lost.

Now I am drawn to dead sites
by nothing but their peace
and chronicles, knowing my cold fault
of *ennui*, the morose search
continuing for a pillage of images,
a loot of dross and old stone.
There is only a thin consolation
of language to fit a picture,
the dry sustenance of craft.

III

It seems a good moment
for stillness — to cut those lights,
to shut off the dance, and bring
the revellers to this wall
above the ruin. Time and decay
combine to shrivel our fleeting
merriment, our poor structures
for celebration, across the toppled
century of Wordsworth's hopes.

I have felt no Presence
in this place, no sense of something
beyond us. But I have felt
a great loneliness here, coming
like melancholy at dusk
in other ruins, like grief
within the silence...
as if we knew, and had always known
how truly alone we were.

Mrs Pankhurst's granddaughter

I see her often
in places where the blinds
are no longer drawn, where light
comes flooding into rooms.

Her clothes are simple, cotton and denim,
and her mind is excellent. She knows Schopenhauer
is not a brand of lager.
She dislikes people who resemble Monday morning
on legs, who have the charm of ferrets.
She has wiped out coffee mornings, Tupperware
    parties, sitting with other people's babies,
    lectures on decorum, small talk, gossip,
    possessions, playing second fiddle to men.

She is a sex grenade
hurled out of the dust
of Victorian diaries, and the frightened lust
of her long-dead sisters.

'I bet you think I'm shocking,' she says,
stroking my grey hair in the refectory
as I smile with pleasure
as she drinks her pint
and puffs on a thin cigar.
'On the contrary,' I reply;
'Where have you been hiding for centuries?'

Twilight in the library

I have not come within their frozen
North, but we all go there
sometime. The entry visa
is age and complete silence
broken only by pages turning.
On a wall is a fitting print
of old people drowsy in Salem.
It takes months of visits, scanning
curled copies of *Punch*
or *Harper's Bazaar*, to reserve your seat.

I offer the old men tobacco
for a roll; they accept me tardily
into the room. They take turns
to keep the tiers of racks tidy
and journals in their proper slots.
                    They trail
bleak lifetimes behind them...
and cough and cough. The Elder
has a red nose and silver stubble,
his magnifier races across *The Times*
and *Guardian*. He is the group's
intellectual, full of useless facts,
making notes in a secret pad
and scribbling faster as closing-time comes.

Rain drips down the sooted panes.
The Elder wheezes over a magazine
while his cronies grunt and sleep, creaking
into December, warming themselves
against hot pipes, propped at the long tables.

There is a sense of all the days ending,
a reluctance to face the night
as the lights come on in the precinct
and a keeper points to the clock.

Cardiff: August 6th '81

The disarmers cluster in the rain
outside Bute's folly
while the soldiers grin at them
lolling among their tanks and guns.

No one sees the irony.
On the day Hiroshima was wasted
we are given a military tattoo
of steel and heavy weapons.

A boy admires the latest rifle
and sits in a fighter cockpit;
his sister carries a plastic union jack
the size of a handkerchief.
He is fodder for another day
when she will wave him goodbye.

In St Mary Street I watch the armour
stop traffic as soldiers trundle
their light tanks with muddy tracks,
pennants on the aerials stiffly wet —
the drivers serious and the captains
smiling proudly from their turrets.

At least they come in peace
on the day Hiroshima was burned,
their memories cut out
and their conduct impeccable.
But if we gave them any trouble
would they still smile at us?

Breaking the past

'I was up in Dowlais yesterday,'
I said to my father.
In a blink he had a picture of the wreck:
'Not much doing there now?'

Not much doing there now....
His words slid the old screen
back onto my mind:
one shattered corner of our century,
a landscape like a warning to the future —

rust, broken neon flickering,
an oildrum floating in a pool
its rainbow slick spreading on top;
blown viaducts, dead pitwheels, more rust,
trains choked with nettle, wind howling
through engine-sheds, chickweed in cracked
cement; slag and scrub under tamping rain,
toppled stacks and fallen Salems,
the black alps oozing filth.

All the scars of enterprise abandoned
in the silence of an armistice
through a battlefield plundered down to its gut
by scrambling ramrods. A Somme
where men looted and ran, leaving
their habitual print of indifference,
leaving
an enormous sadness.

The worn images on the screen
faded, and my father's words
with them.... What the makers
of our destiny did not break
was the bonding spirit.
                    Community and love
still thrived on these desolate rims,
the hope never quite leaked away,
the fortitude that made them.

Green order, soft and fertile to us,
would come again, real daylight
splash the townships and fields,
horizons clear of pillage.
It was our covenant with tomorrow.

I knew I was tired
of the Past, that great
haunting — and guilty
because I was tired.

Louis MacNeice in the 'Cock'

Great Portland Street at opening time, at dusk
when the jewellers and rag-traders locked up
and the broadcasters filed to their booze.
He was there most nights when the Third
didn't stick his brilliance in a cubicle
with knobs, buttons, switches and dials
waiting for a red light to flick.
On summer afternoons he watched cricket at Lord's.

Everything about him was dark:
he wore a black leather coat
standing alone at the bar
like a rich romantic French actor
or a matador taking his ease.
I hoped Auden would come in from New York
to break his silence, making
a double flash of glamour
among the clerks and tartan panels.

I never approached him, being nothing much
at the Old Beeb, and he
seemed formidable, with a known flair
for testiness, and a cold-blooded gift
for disdain — leaning back, holding a glass
and looking at the world from a distance
through half-closed eyes. It was an aloof
hooded glance, to keep people away
and his distinction intact. It was what
Spender called a superior head
with lancing eyes sizing you up.
I thought then he did not belong,
that somehow he would not grow old.

He was *in* life, yet above it —
a shocked observer pretending to be amused.
In the Cock Tavern long ago
his *Autumn Journal* was inside his head
and his eyes seemed fixed on some débâcle:
　'Crumbling between the fingers, under the feet,
　Crumbling behind the eyes,
　Their world gives way and dies
　And something twangs and breaks at the end of the
　　　　　　　　　　　　　　　　　street.'

Benefits

1 Signing-on

The dole lines remind me of travellers
waiting for tickets in a station.
We shuffle, smoke, look at watches.
Behind glass, the young clerks are polite,
another breed from their bleak forerunners
as they listen to woe, bewilderment, near-panic.
The man in front of me
is stricken, spluttering his distress
through the glass. It will take time
to sort out his life on paper.

I put my signature on the Giro release
and count small blessings, remembering
the skeletons of Victorian workhouses
seen from the windows of trains
where life, as a meaningful function, stopped —
the inmates like vegetables in darkness
slurping toothless on gruel.

At Gabalfa, it is not too desolate,
it doesn't look like a tragedy
in the bright morning sun.
But we are, somehow, separate —
outside the stream.

2   The skint trap

The Cross Inn is flooded with this sun
exposing its rickety makeshift saloon
of cardboard and tin, linoleum floor
scuffed to a bare hessian.
It was jacked up in a week, fifty years ago.

The jobless shoot pool, slamming
balls into pockets, or they watch
an Indian spinner on the screen
tying an Englishman in knots.
Some ration their intake of ale,
then leave; some linger, sipping it
like champagne through the endless hour.
We sample imitation meat pies,
play darts, dominoes, shove ha'penny, crib.
The young ones are learning the fatal skills
                    of boredom and trivia.

Here, in the trap, there is only resignation,
an acceptance of promises unkept
and a knowledge of perfidy; a dimness
of sinking spirits held tight at the tolerable.
What goes on inside their heads
                    I can only guess at.

Catching the night sleeper

Paddington in late March
when solitaries like to travel,
waiting under its Brunel masterpiece.
Fleets of taxis jam the rank
and the mail-trains are loaded.
Tramps squat in their allotted quarter
by the warm-air vents, rolling cigarettes.

Cornwall is my destination
as far away as dawn,
but I'm having a small breakdown
standing up, and cannot decide
whether to go to the buffet
let alone Penzance.
                    I slide two lifters
through an aperture out of their pack
and pop them like mints
into my mouth, washing them down
with Scotch from a flask.

Stress for no reason
is a puzzle I've not solved.
It has something to do with stations,
departures and farewells
when faces we love disappear from view.
At Paddington my anxiety
sees women in long coats
waving handkerchiefs at soldiers
as the train pulls away.
They watch it out of sight,
then turn round and start to weep.
A moment later they have gone,

leaving only a scent of lavender and mothballs
hanging in the dust and smoke of Platform Ten.

An amplified voice is droning West Country stops.
Time now to board the Cornish sleeper
with my kitbag and sandwiches,
paperback Snow and crosswords.
Traces of yesterday still flicker
on the cracked screen of my mind.
I jerk myself upright to face
what we call reality, as the wheels turn
and the diesel hoots, and I sit alone
by the window inside my small breakdown.

Llandrindod Wells was not built
for disturbance, or republican cabals.
Jacobins were shown the way out of town.
It was a rendezvous for safe
Radnor Tories in clerical grey
dipping their bowlers to convention,
taking the spa waters....

In the Metropole
Wilfred Owen and Lawrence of Arabia
stayed, lingering overnight
on the roads to their peculiar destinies.

I sit in an opulent conservatory
waiting for my teapot and Osborne biscuit
under fanned-out silks slung below glass
with light pouring down on the peach carpet.

It is a last shred of Georgian elegance
ringed by Victorian frippery
and the pomp of their bloated day
where now the white paint is flaking
off splintered trellis and wicker chair.

A mingled blessing: the odd imprint
an empire leaves, like a foreign stamp
on an old card, kept for rarity's sake;
the mark of its careless passing,
the desolation of its remnant.
In corners stand its gifts of faded
splendour, on lawns stand its rusted guns.